MW01516695

# *where* PRAISE *begins*

## A WORSHIP CHOIR COLLECTION

*Arranged by* GERON DAVIS
*and* BRADLEY KNIGHT

*Featuring the songs of:*
RANDY PHILLIPS, DAN DEAN, DAVE CLARK AND GERON DAVIS

*Orchestrated by* BRADLEY KNIGHT

## lillenas
PUBLISHING COMPANY

lillenas.com

# CONTENTS

# Where Praise Begins

Words and Music by
GERON DAVIS, TONY WOOD
and DAVE CLARK
*Arr. by Geron Davis
and Bradley Knight*

**1** Funky Pop Feel ♩ = 87

**SOLO**

There's a cry___ that's ring-ing from the heart-

10

- beat of a seek - ing gen - er - a - tion,

LADIES *unis.*
*mp*

From a

A♭m    B♭♯9/7    E♭m

12

call-ing for ___ His pres - ence ___ and His

seek-ing gen - er - a - tion. ___

A♭m    B♭♯9/7    E♭m

14

ho - ly pow'r - to fall ___ on ev -'ry na - tion. ___    There are

A♭m    B♭♯9/7    E♭m    C♭maj7    G♭/B♭

words of wor - ship ris - ing from peo-ple on their knees, the

song of the re-deemed, and this is where I wan-na be. Where

CHOIR *div.*

Where

SOLO *continues on melody and may ad lib*

praise be-gins, there is hope and heal - ing. Where

**22**

praise be-gins,___ You'll find His love___ re-deem-ing.

C m7  E♭/G  A♭2  B♭

**24**

Noth-ing is___ im-pos-si-ble___ when we en-ter in.___

B♭m/D♭  A♭/C  A♭m/C♭  E♭/B♭

**2nd time to Coda** ⊕
*(page 11, meas. 41)*

**26**

I wan-na be___ where praise___ be-gins.

**2nd time to Coda** ⊕
*(page 11, meas. 41)*

A♭2  B♭sus  E♭  C7(#9)

**3**

28

He's gon-na be___ where praise_____ be-gins.____

A♭2    B♭sus    E♭2

30

Come in - to___ His pres - ence___ with thanks -

E♭m

31

*SOLO may ad lib*

giv - ing and___ in - to___ His courts with sing - in'.____

A♭m    B♭⁺⁹₇    E♭m

33
Make a joy - ful noise, clap your
A♭m
B♭7♯9
E♭m
35
hands and keep the hal - le-lu - jah's ring - in'.
A♭m
B♭7♯9
E♭m
C♭maj7
G♭/B♭
37
Two or three to-geth - er can bring His pres - ence near. One
A♭m
C♭maj7
B♭m7
A♭m7
G♭maj7/B♭

39

**4**

**D.S. al Coda**
*(page 7, meas. 20)*

mind and one ac-cord___ will chase___ a - way all doubt and fear.  Where

A♭m/F

B♭7/♯5

**D.S. al Coda**
*(page 7, meas. 20)*

CODA    **5**

41    SOLO

He's gon - na be___ where praise_____ be - gins.

CODA    A♭2

B♭sus

42

mp

Bro - ken bod - ies and___ lives___ find a new song to sing,___

mp

G♭

G♭/F

E♭m7

G♭/D♭

G♭/C♭

mp

44
mf
to sing, yeah!
C♭maj9/D♭
46
mp
Bro-ken chains on the ground, cap-tives freed and re - deemed,
G♭
G♭/F
E♭m7
G♭/D♭
G♭/C♭
48
6
f
re-deemed. Where praise be-gins,
B♭7sus
E♭2
E♭/G

51

there is hope___ and heal - ing. Where praise be-gins,___

A♭2   E2   E/G♯

53

there is hope___ and heal - ing. Where praise be-gins,___ You'll

A2   B   C♯m7   E/G♯

55

find His love___ re-deem - ing. Noth-ing is___ im-pos - si - ble___

A2   B   Bm/D   A/C♯

**57**

when we en - ter in. I wan-na be where praise be-gins.

A m / C    E / B    A 2    B sus

**59**

He's gon-na be where praise be-gins.

E    C#7 #9    A 2    B sus

**61**

SOLO *may ad lib to end*

C#m  B/D#  E    E  F#m  E/G#    A maj7  B C#m7

Where praise be - gins.

Where praise be - gins.

Where praise be - gins.

C♯m B/D♯ E    E F♯m E/G♯    Amaj7 B C♯m7

Where praise be - gins.

C♯m B/D♯ E    E F♯m E/G♯    Amaj7 B C♯m7

Where praise be - gins.

C♯m B/D♯ E    E F♯m E/G♯    Amaj7 B C♯m7

Where praise be - gins.

Where praise be - gins.

I wan-na be, I wan-na be, yeah!

C#m B/D# E E F#m E/G# E/G# E/A

I wan-na be, I wan-na be, yeah, where praise be-gins!

C#m B/D# E E F#m E/G# E/G# E/A E/G# E/A

(8)

# Overtaken

Words and Music by
DAN DEAN and DEVIN DEAN
*Arr. by Geron Davis
and Bradley Knight*

**9** Driving Rock ♩ = 131

Look-ing___ back___ at___ where___ I've___ been,___ I can___ clear - ly___ see___

_Your_ hand at each and ev - 'ry turn that I have faced.

And e-ven when I felt a - lone,

now I see that I was wrong. You've been there be - side

C   Am   G

F   C   G

F2   C   Am7

me all the way. And ev-'ry - where I look, I see Your bless-ings com - ing af - ter me. No place that I can hide from mer - cy's hand.

10

Lyrics:
I am o-ver-tak - en by Your

mer - cy and Your grace. I'm o-ver-tak-

-en and I just can't get a - way. I am o-ver-tak-

46

-en; I've been caught by heav - en's hand. And Your prom-

F

$\frac{C}{E}$

F

49

**2nd time to Coda** ⊕
*(page 26, meas. 81)*

-ise is I'll nev - er be for-sak - en.

$\frac{F^2}{D}$

$\frac{C}{E}$

$F^2$

**2nd time to Coda** ⊕
*(page 26, meas. 81)*

52

11

O-ver - tak - en!

C

$F\sharp\frac{4}{2}$

$F^2$

C

Com-ing___ in___ and___ go - ing___ out,

I can___ see,___ with - out___ a___ doubt,___ bless-ings___ on___ my___ left___

___ and___ on___ my___ right.___ And

e-ven when I lose my way, You're there be-side me night

and day. I can't es-cape Your fa - vor in my life.

Don't wan-na run, but if

74

I tried, there'd be no - where for me to hide.

G

C/F

G

77

_f_

Ev - 'ry - where I turn I see Your face.

_f_

C/F

C/F

79

**12**

**D.S. al Coda**
_(page 21, meas. 37)_

I am

F♯4/2   F2   F♯4/2   F2

**D.S. al Coda**
_(page 21, meas. 37)_

**CODA**

81

I'm o - ver - tak - en

**CODA**

F2    C    F2

84  **13**

*sub. p*

Caught by love when I

*sub. p*

C    F2    C

*sub. p*

87

had lost my way,

F2/D    C/E    F2

Lyrics:

90 caught and__ nev - er__ want__ to get__ a - way.__

93 Caught by__ love__ when__ I__ had__ lost__ my__ way,__

96 caught and__ nev - er__ want__

**99**

to\_\_ get a \- way.\_\_

F2/D          C/E          F2

**102**  *f*

Caught by\_\_ love\_\_ when I\_\_ had\_\_ lost\_\_ my\_\_ way,\_\_

mel. *f*

C          F2/D          C/E

*f*

**105**          **14**

caught and\_\_ nev \- er want\_\_ to\_\_ get a \- way.\_\_

F2          C          F2/D

Whoa, I am o-ver-tak - en by Your mer - cy and Your grace. I'm o-ver-tak - en and I just can't get a - way.

118
I am o - ver - tak - en; I've been
G
Am7
F
121
caught by heav - en's hand. And Your prom - ise is I'll nev -
C/E
F
F2/D
124
- er be for-sak - en. I'm o - ver - tak -
C/E
F2
G

127
en
C
F#4 2
F2
C
130
I'm o-ver - tak - en
F
C
F#4 2
F2
C
134
(15)
O - ver - tak - en!
F
C
(16)

# There Was a Lamb

Words and Music by
GERON DAVIS and TONY WOOD
*Arr. by Geron Davis
and Bradley Knight*

Long be-fore E-den had seen its first light, long be-fore man took his first breath of life, God, in Your wis-dom, had writ-ten a per-fect

A²  E  E

plan. Oh, long be-fore man heard the temp-

A  A#4/2  A²  A⁶  E

-ter's sly voice, long be-fore he made that fate-ful wrong choice,

E  A²  A²

**21**

*cast from the gar - den, a gulf be-tween God and___ man,___*

E       E       A       A $^{\#4}_{2}$

**24**

*yes, long be-fore there was a world,___ there was a Lamb.*

A $^2$   A $^6$    F#m $^7$       B $_{sus}$

**27** | **16**

CHOIR *div.*
*f*

*O great Re-deem - er, with*

*f*

E       E       $\frac{E}{A}$

*f*

such ho-ly love, choos-ing that You'd give Your-self to save us,

God of the a - ges be-com-ing the Sav-ior of man.

Now we walk____ in free-dom that can-not be tak-en;

we stand in faith___ that can-not be shak-en, so un-de-served,___ but

giv - en a sec - ond chance. All be-cause___

___ be-fore there was a world,___ there was a Lamb.

**17**

Lord, we are hum - bled that we know Your grace, and

we'll bow for - ev - er to give You our praise for the

thorns in Your head, and the wounds in Your nail scarred hands,

and that long be-fore there was a world,

there was a Lamb.

Slain be-fore the ver-y foun-da-tion of time,

be-cause of Your grace, Your love, and Your mer-cy di-

vine. O great Re-deem-er, with

40

such ho-ly love, choos-ing that You'd give Your-self to save us,

God of the a - ges be-com-ing the Sav-ior of man.

Now we walk in free-dom that can-not be tak-en;

we stand in faith___ that can-not be shak-en, so un-de-served,___ but

giv-en a sec-ond chance. All be-cause___

___ be-fore there was a world,_____ long be-fore there was a world,___ thank You God, be-fore there was a world,

there was a Lamb.

# Gentle Breeze

Words and Music by
**DAN DEAN**
*Arr. by Geron Davis
and Bradley Knight*

**20** Tenderly ♩ = 60

TENOR SOLO

Feel-ing like___ a des-ert burn-ing in___ the sum-mer sun,___ parched and dry,___ I qui-et-ly___ cry___ for

8
sweet re-lief to come. 'Cause Lord, You see, the soul in me is
G
A sus
D2/F♯
10
yearn - ing for a gen - tle breeze,
D
D/F♯
G2
D/F♯
12
bring-ing sweet re-fresh - ing I so bad - ly need.
3
Em7
D/F♯
A(add4)
14
Yes - ter-day's re-fresh - ing brought a false se-cu - ri-ty that
D
G/D

deep in-side I thought that I would make it through the heat.

I was wrong, but now I long for gen-tle breez - es I

have known to blow a-gain and bring me sweet re-

**21**

lief.____ Gen - tle breeze____ from heav - en, blow a-

CHOIR *div.*
*mp*

Gen - tle breeze____ from heav - en, blow a-

*mp*

A sus    D    D/F#

cross my__ soul,____ cool and sweet__ re-fresh - ing rain on

cross my__ soul,____ cool and sweet__ re-fresh - ing rain on__

G#4/2  G    A sus    A

26

_me. Sooth - ing Spir - it, fill___ me 'til I_

_me. Sooth - ing Spir - it, fill___ me 'til I_

D          D          D/F#

28

_o - ver - flow.___ Gen-tle breeze___ of love, bring rest to me._

_o - ver - flow.___ Gen-tle breeze___ of love, bring rest to me._

G #4/2 G          D/A          A          D  A  Bm  D/F#

48

36

I was wrong, and now I long for gen-tle breez-es I

Ooo.

A sus   D²/F#   D   D/F#

38

have known to blow a-gain and bring me sweet re-

Ah.

G   C   G/B

23
40
- lief, yeah.
Gen - tle breeze from heav - en, blow a -
mp
Gen - tle breeze from heav - en, blow a -
mp
A sus
D
D/F♯
42
cross my soul,
cool and sweet re-fresh - ing rain on
cross my soul,
cool and sweet re-fresh - ing rain on
G ♯4/2
G
A sus
A

44
me. Sooth-ing Spi - rit. 'Til I
me. Sooth-ing Spir - it, fill me 'til I
D A7sus D D/F♯
46
o - ver - flow. Gen - tle breeze of love,
o - ver - flow. Gen - tle breeze of love,
G♯4/2 G D/A A

gen - tle breeze____ of love,____

gen - tle breeze____ of love____

Bm    A    G    D/F#    Em7

let   your love.____    Gen - tle breeze____ of

bring   rest   to   me.

A7sus    D    A    Bm    D/F#

love, won't You come,

Ooo.

G                           D       A       Bm      D/F#

*Rit.*

bring rest to me.

Em7                Asus                  D

*Rit.*

# The Love of God

Words and Music by
**FREDERICK H. LEHMAN**
*Arr. by Geron Davis*
*and Bradley Knight*

**24** Gently ♩ = 72

CHOIR *unis.*

The love of\_\_\_ God is great-er far_____ than tongue or\_\_\_ pen can ev-er

**12**

tell. It goes be - yond the high-est star,\_\_\_ and reach-es\_\_\_

C    C    C sus    C

**15**

to the low-est hell. The guilt-y\_\_ pair bowed down with

mel.

$\frac{G}{B}$    $\frac{F}{A}$    C    F 2

**18**

care; God gave His Son\_\_\_\_\_ to\_\_ win. His err-ing\_\_\_

$\frac{C^2}{E}$    $\frac{C\,sus}{D}$    C 2

child He rec-on - ciled, and par-doned from his

sin. Ah, ah.

Could we with ink the o-cean fill, and were the

31

skies of parch-ment made, were ev-'ry_ stalk on earth a

$\frac{G}{C}$  C  C  C sus

34

quill,_ and ev-'ry_ man a scribe by trade, to write the_

mel.

C  $\frac{G}{B}$  $\frac{F}{A}$  C

37

love of God a - bove would drain the o - cean_

F 2  $\frac{C}{E}$  $\frac{C sus}{D}$

dry.\_\_\_\_ Nor could the\_\_ scroll con - tain the

whole, though stretched from sky\_\_\_\_\_ to\_\_\_\_

**26**

sky.

MEN *div.* O love of God,\_\_\_ how rich and pure,

ALTO
O

46
Add SOPRANOS
It shall for -
love of God.
how meas - ure - less and strong!
F2
C
E
48
ev - er - more en - dure.
Hal - le lu - jah! Hal - le - lu -
Hal - le - lu - jah! Hal - le - lu -
TENOR
BASS Hal - le - lu - jah!
F2
C2
E

27

Hal - le - lu - jah! Hal - le - lu - jah!

- jah! Hal - le - lu - jah!

- jah! Hal - le - lu - jah!

Hal - le - lu - jah! Hal - le - lu - jah!

$F\frac{9}{6}$

$\frac{C\,2}{E}$

*f*

O love of God, how rich and pure, how meas-ure-

*f*

$\frac{C\,m}{E\flat}$ $\frac{C\,sus}{D}$ $\frac{C}{E}$

F

$C\,2$ C

less\_\_\_\_\_ and\_\_ strong!\_\_\_ It shall for - ev - - - er-more en-

dure\_\_\_\_ the saints' and an - - gels'\_\_ song. It shall for -

ev - - er-more en - dure\_\_\_ the saints' and an - - - gels'\_\_

62

song.

O love of God,___ how rich and pure,___ how meas-ure-less and___ strong!

O love of God,___ how rich and pure, how meas-ure-less and___ strong!

ALTO

O love of God.

O love of God, how rich and pure, how meas-ure-less and strong!

A m7    F 2

*Add* SOPRANOS

It shall for - ev - er - more en -

Hal - le lu -

Hal - le - lu -

TENOR

A m7    F 2

dure.
Hal - le - lu - jah!
80
- jah! Hal - le - lu - jah! Hal - le - lu -
- jah! Hal - le - lu - jah! Hal - le - lu -
BASS Hal - le - lu - jah! Hal - le - lu - jah!
C/E
F2
Hal - le - lu - jah!
82
Rit.
- jah!
- jah!
Hal - le - lu - jah!
C/E
F2
Rit.
C2

# Your Love

Words and Music by
RANDY PHILLIPS
and JOHN RAGSDALE
*Arr. by Geron Davis
and Bradley Knight*

9
2nd time: SOLO may ad lib
like an o - cean,
wide as it is deep.
A7sus
A7
A7sus
mf
12
Your love,
like a riv - er
of
A7
D7sus
D7
15
mer - cy flow-in' con - tin - u - al - ly.
Your love,
A7sus
A7
3

Your love,_____ a - maz - ing love.

Your love, love.

SOLO *may ad lib to end*

Your love, like a moun - tain

ris - ing___ from the___ deep.___ Your love,___

like an ea - gle with wings that wrap a-round___ me.

Your love,___ Your love,___ a - maz - ing

33
32
love.
A7sus
A7
cresc.
35
f
Can't un - der - stand it, can't com - pre - hend it,
A (no3)
G (no3)
A (no3)
C (no3)
37
noth - ing in all of this world can ev - er end it. Your love,
A (no3)

39

a - maz - ing___ luh -

D7sus          D7

41

- hove.___                    Your love,

A7sus            A7

**2nd time to Coda ⊕**
*(page 76, meas. 71)*

43

Your love,___        a - maz - ing

E#9 7          D7

**2nd time to Coda ⊕**
*(page 76, meas. 71)*

33

love.

Your love,

A⁷sus

A⁷

like an o - cean,  wide as  it is  deep.

A⁷sus

A⁷

A⁷sus

mf

sim.

Your love,  like a riv - er of

A⁷

D⁷sus

D⁷

mer - cy flow-in' con - tin - u - al - ly. Your love,

Your love, a - maz - ing love.

Your love, like a moun - tain

ris - ing from the deep. Your love,

like an ea - gle with

wings that wrap a - round me. Your love,

**34**

Your love,_____ a - maz - ing

love.

Well!_____

E♯9/7

D7

A7sus

A7

cresc.

**D.S. al Coda**
*(page 70, meas. 35)*

**D.S. al Coda**
*(page 70, meas. 35)*

CODA

Your a-maz-ing love, yeah, yeah!

Your a-maz-ing love!

Can't un - der - stand it,

can't com - pre - hend it, noth - ing in all of this world

can ev - er end it. Your love,

92
a - maz - ing luh - hove.
D 7
sim.
A 7sus
94
Your love, Your love, a - maz - ing
A 7
E #9 7
D 7
97
love. Your love, Your love,
A 7sus
A 7
E #9 7

100

a - maz - ing love.

Your love,

D 7

A 7sus

A 7

103

Your love, a - maz - ing love.

E 7#9

D 7

A (no 3)

106

Love, yeah!

# Because of That Blood

Words and Music by
RANDY PHILLIPS
and MARK HARRIS
*Arr. by Geron Davis
and Bradley Knight*

**37** Soulful R&B Feel ♩ = 81

MALE SOLO

Earn your

way,___ hey,___ that's the les-son that___ we're taught, but I___ know things e-ter-nal can't be sold and can't be bought. A-maz-ing

grace hey, is some-thing I could nev-er hold, and I

know love and mer-cy are out-side of my con-trol.

13

But I'm re-mind - - - ed of__ a ran - som, paid__

CHOIR *div.*

*mp*

Ooo.

*mp*

D♭

Fm⁷

15

be - yond__ my worth, on a hill out-side__ the cit - y, where heav-

B♭m⁷

A♭/C

D♭2(no3)

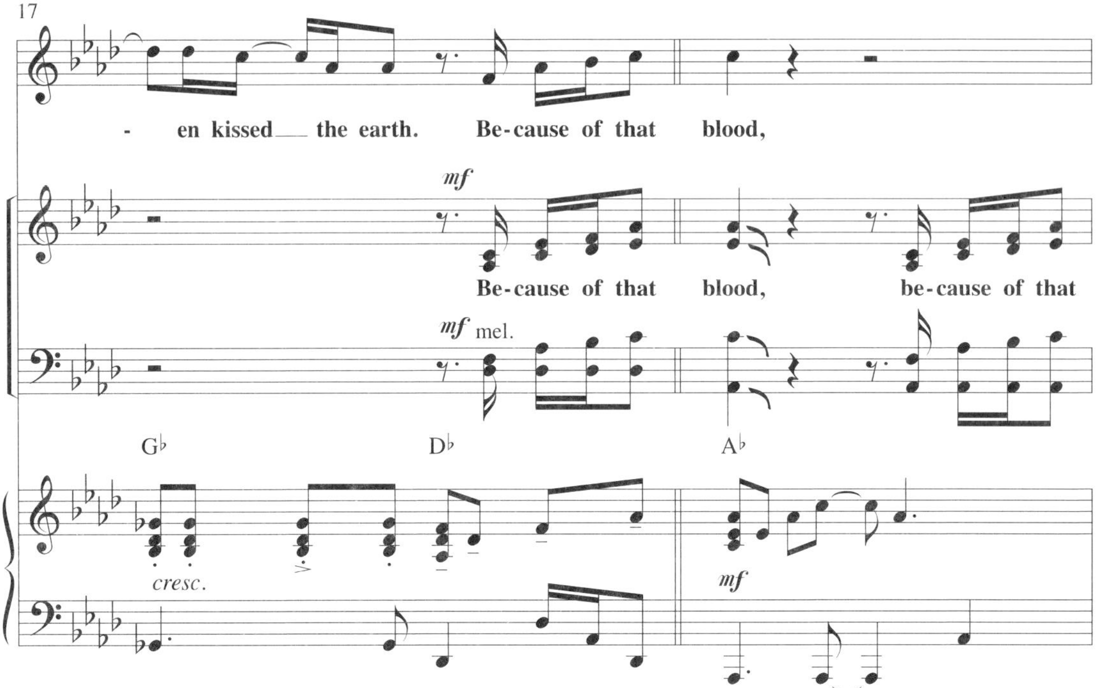
17
- en kissed the earth. Be-cause of that blood,
mf
Be-cause of that blood, be-cause of that
mf mel.
G♭
D♭
A♭
cresc.
mf

19
be-cause of that tree, be-cause of that mer - cy
tree, be-cause of that mer - cy
B♭m7
A♭/C
D♭2(no3)

21
pour - ing o - ver me, be - cause of that grace I've been set
pour - ing o - ver me, be - cause of that grace I've been set
G♭ D♭ Fm7
23
free. Be - cause of You, Je - sus,
free. Be - cause of You, Je - sus, I have been re - deemed.
B♭sus B♭ D♭ G♭
(♭)
dim.

25

39

oh, thank You, Lord. Some be-

27

lieve they can make it on their own, but on-

Some be-lieve, ooo.

Fm7

Gb2 Db2

Fm7 Bbm7

-ly in the end to find they're real - ly not that strong. But I be-

But I be-

lieve, hoo, if I choose to live by faith, that God

lieve, ooo.

will give me strength to make it each and ev - 'ry day.

We are lost with-out a Sav - ior, to save

We are lost!

us from our - selves. It's on -

Save us from our - selves.

*mp*

*mp*

B♭m7

A♭/C

38

**40**

- ly by the grace of God that we can live to tell.

*mf*

Ah,

*mf*

D♭2(no 3)

G♭

*cresc.*

40

SOLO *may ad lib*

Hey!

PRAISE TEAM *mf*

Be - cause of that blood,_____ be-

*cresc.*

be-cause of that blood, be-cause of that

*cresc.*

D♭        A♭

*cresc.*

*mf*

42

cause of that tree.____ Ooo,

tree, be-cause of that mer - cy____

B♭m7        A♭/C        D♭

44
ooo.
Be - cause of that grace,
pour-ing o - ver me,
be-cause of that
grace
I've been set
G♭
D♭/F
E♭m
D♭
F m7
46
I've been set free.
Ooo.
free.
Be-cause of You,
Je-sus, I have been
re - deemed.
B♭sus
B♭
D♭2
G♭2

**41**

SOLO
*f*

Who of us can say that we are wor-

cresc.

A♭    G♭

-thy of the blood of Je - sus Christ?

The
TENORS *only*

B♭m7    A♭/C    D♭#4/2    D♭2

52
All that we can do is sim - ply of -
blood of Je - sus Christ.
Add BASSES
D♭ ♯4 2
D♭2 F
G♭
54
- fer Him our all by lay - ing down our lives.
By lay - ing down our lives.
B♭m7
B♭sus
B♭

**42**

Oh, be-cause of that blood, be-cause of that

Ooo,

E♭sus    A♭

tree, be-cause of that mer - cy, Lord, it's

ooo.

B♭m7    A♭2/C    D♭

60

pour - ing o - ver me,_____ be - cause of that

PRAISE TEAM

Be -

*mf cresc.*

Pour - ing o - ver me._____ Be - cause of that

*mf cresc.*

G♭    D♭/F    E♭m    D♭

*f*

61

grace    I've been set    free.    Be - cause of You,

cause of that grace,_____    I've been set free._____

*f*

grace    I've been set    free.

*f*

Fm7    B♭sus    B♭

63

SOLO *may ad lib to the end*

Je-sus, I have been re - deemed.

Be - cause of that blood,_____ be-

be-cause of that blood, be-cause of that

D♭2    G♭2                    A♭

65

cause of that tree._____ Ooo,

tree, be-cause of that mer-cy_____

B♭m          A♭/C          D♭2

ooo.

Be - cause of that grace,

pour-ing o - ver me, be-cause of that grace I've been set

G♭   D♭/F   E♭m   D♭   F m7

I've been set free. Ooo.

free. Be-cause of You, Je - sus, I have been re - deemed.

B♭sus   B♭   D♭2   G♭

Be - cause of that grace,___

be-cause of that grace

I've been set

I've been set free.___

Ooo.___

free.

Be-cause of You, Je-sus, I have been re-deemed.

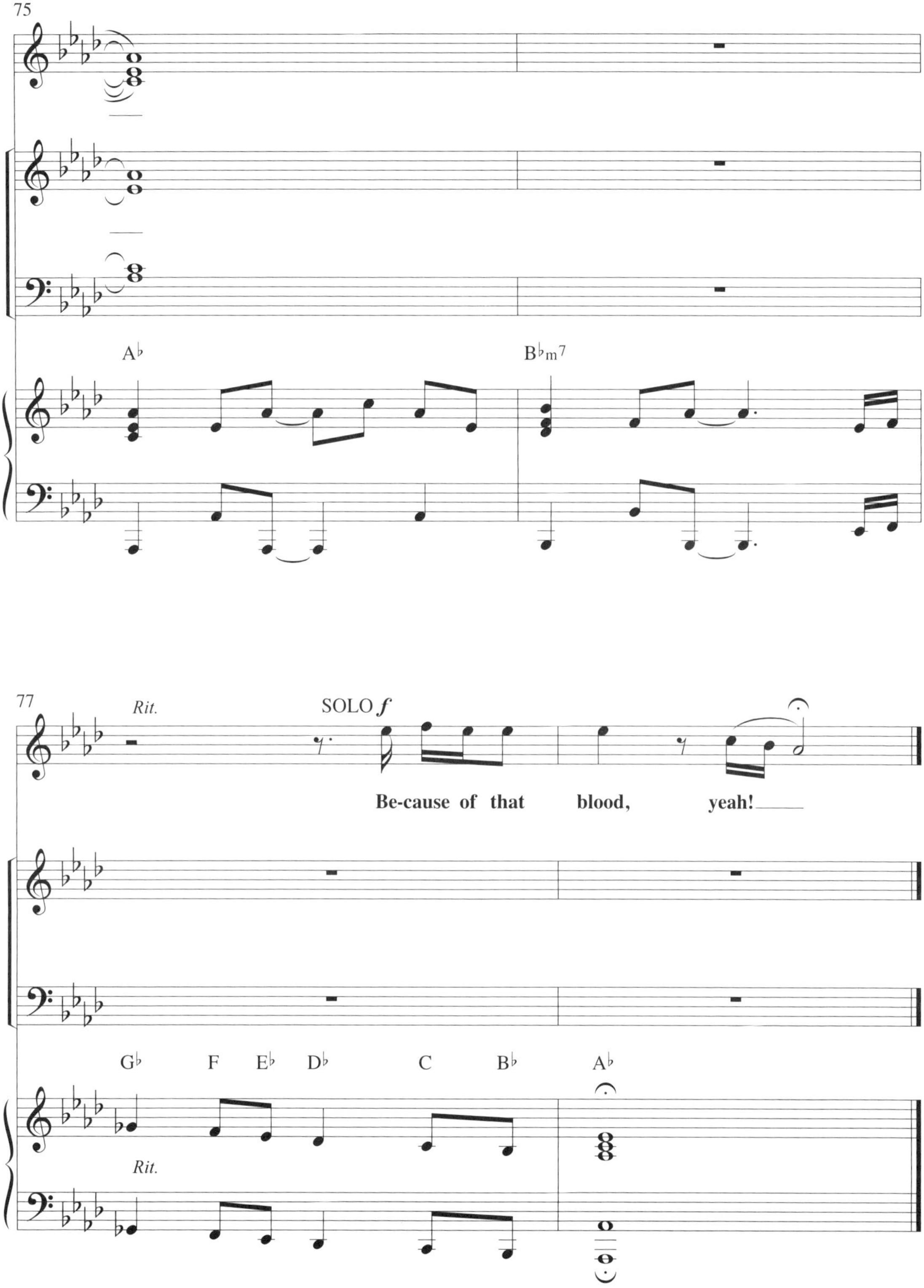
75
A♭
B♭m7
77
Rit.
SOLO f
Be-cause of that blood, yeah!
G♭ F E♭ D♭ C B♭
A♭
Rit.

# Heart, Soul, Mind and Strength

Words and Music by
**GERON DAVIS**
*Arr. by Geron Davis
and Bradley Knight*

**With my heart, soul, mind, and strength**

**I will wor - ship You, I will wor - ship You.**

Lyrics (with chords):

**8**
Giv-ing You my ev-'ry-thing,
B sus    B    E    B/D#

**10**
I will wor-ship You. Lord, I will wor-ship You.
C#m7   E/B   E/G#   A2   E/B   B

**12** | 44 |
Ho-ly God, You are the Lord of all,
E    B    B/D#    E sus    E

who gave ev - 'ry-thing___ for___ me.___

Sac - ri - fic - ing heav - en's prec - ious___ Lamb,___

You gave it all___ so will-ing-ly,___ so how

21

can I___ give___ an-y-thing less to-day?___ Sur-

F#m7    E/A    B sus    B

23

| 45 |

ren-der___-ing___ ev-er-y-thing I___ say.___ With my

F#m7    E/A    B sus    B    B/D#

25

heart, soul, mind,___ and___ strength___ I will wor-ship You,___

E2    B/D#    C#m7    E/B

mp

27
I will wor - ship You.
Giv-ing
A2
B sus
29
You my ev - 'ry - thing,
I will wor - ship You.
E2
B/D♯
C♯m7
E/B
E/G♯
31
46
Lord, I will wor - ship You.
A2
E/B
B
E

33
Ho - ly God, You are the Lord of all,
B
B
D♯
E sus
E
35
who gave ev - 'ry-thing for me.
B
B
A
E
G♯
E 2
37
Sac - ri - fic - ing heav - en's pre - cious Lamb,
A
B sus
B

39
You gave it all so will-ing-ly, so how
E/A
A2
B sus
B
41
can I give an-y-thing less to - day? Sur -
E sus/F♯
E/A
B sus
B
43
mf
47
ren - der - ing ev-er-y - thing I say. With my
E sus/F♯
E/A
B sus
B
B/D♯
cresc.

heart, soul, mind, and strength I will wor - ship You,

E     B/D#     C#m7     E/B

*mf*

I will wor - ship You. Giv-ing

A2     Bsus

You my ev - 'ry - thing, I will wor - ship You.

E     B/D#     C#m7     E/B     E/G#

51
48
f
Lord, I will wor - ship You. With my
A
E/B
B
E
C sus
cresc.
53
heart, soul, mind, and strength I will wor - ship You,
F
C/E
Am7 Dm7
F/C
f
55
I will wor - ship You. Giv - ing
B♭2
B♭2/D
C sus
C

57
You my ev - 'ry - thing,
I will wor - ship You.
F
C/E
Dm7
F/C
F/A
59
Lord, I will wor - ship You.
Giv-ing
B♭
F/C
C
F
B♭/D
C/E
61
You my ev - 'ry - thing,
I will wor - ship You.
F
C/E
Dm7
F/C
F/A

Lord,___ I will wor - ship You.___

I will wor - ship You.

# Where Amazing Happens

Words and Music by
DAN DEAN
*Arr. by Geron Davis
and Bradley Knight*

**49** Broadly ♩ = 64

MALE SOLO
*mp*

Stand-ing on the edge of los-ing ev-'ry-thing,

out of op-tions, out of hopes, you've lost your way. Your

hap - py ev - er af - ter did-n't turn out like\_\_\_ you planned,\_\_\_

search - ing for\_\_\_ a sol - id place\_\_\_ to stand.\_\_\_

Look - ing at\_\_\_ the ash - es of\_\_\_ what could have been,\_\_\_

15
can't help won - d'rin' if you fin - 'lly reached the end. Yet
D/F♯ G/B C♯4/2 C
17
3
in this space of weak - ness is where mir - a-cles be-gin;
D/F♯ G2/B C♯4/2 C G/B
19
50
watch and see, the dead can live a-gain. This is where a-
CHOIR div.
mp
This is where a-
mel. mp
Am7 Dsus D

maz - ing___ hap-pens; this is where God steps___ in;___ this is the place___

maz - ing___ hap-pens; this is where God steps___ in;

___ where bro - ken dreams___ can live a-gain.___ When you're to the

Ooo.___ When you're to the

end of____ hope,____ no-where else for you to go,____

end of____ hope,____ no-where else for you to go,____

G D/F# G/B

wel-come to__ a place__ of sec - ond chanc - es;____ this is where a-maz-ing

ooo,_____ this is where a-maz-ing

A m7 G/C D sus D

51

hap - pens. Dawn can nev - er come___ un-less___ there's been

hap - pens.

G sus          G          D/F#                              G/B

___ a night;___          heal - ing can - not come___ with-out___ a ru-

Ooo.___

C #4/2          C          D/F#                              G/B

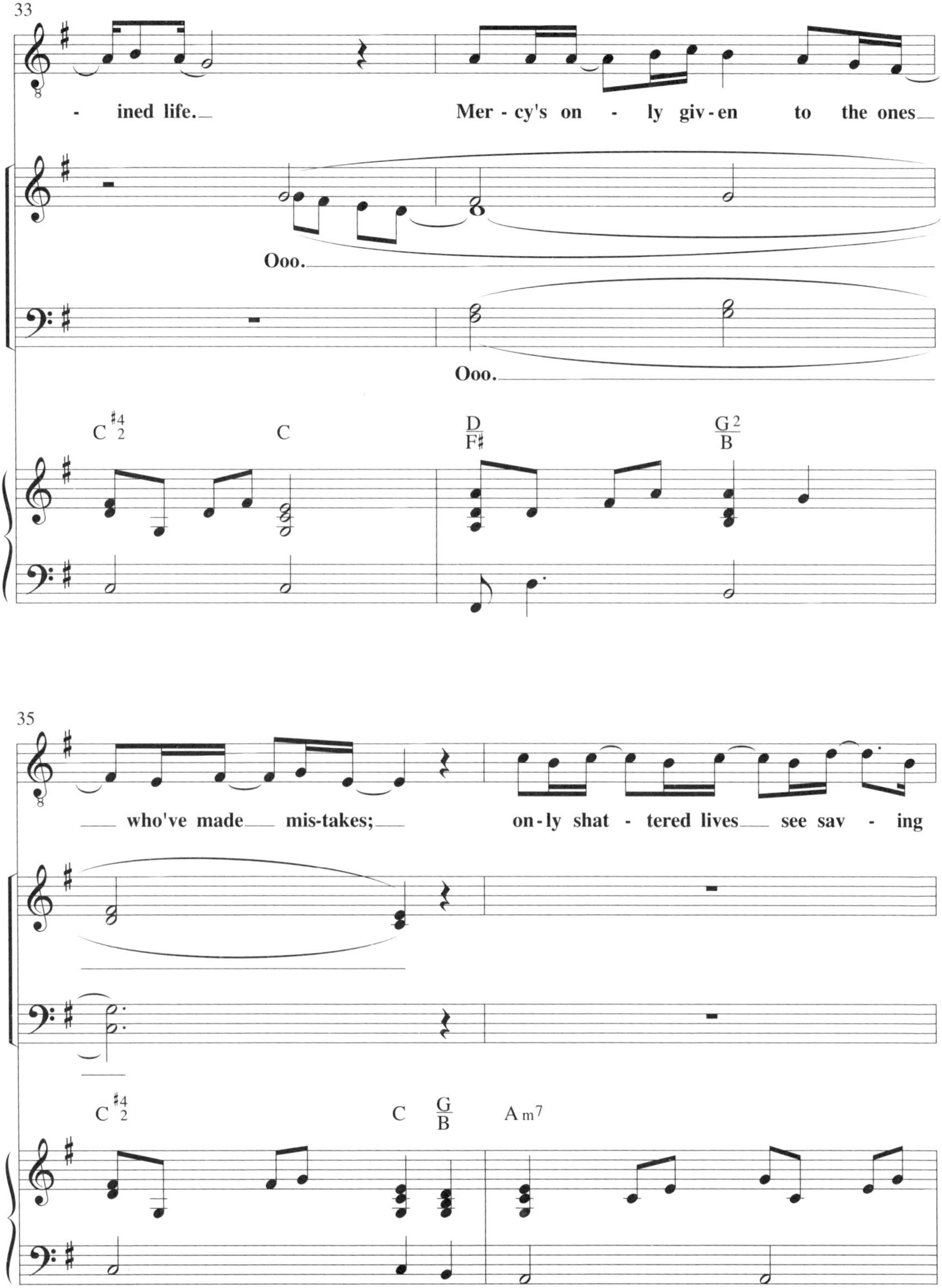
33
- ined life.
Mer - cy's on - ly giv - en to the ones
Ooo.
Ooo.
C#4 2
C
D F#
G2 B
35
who've made mis-takes;
on-ly shat - tered lives see sav - ing
C#4 2
C
G B
Am7

grace.\_\_\_\_ This is where a - maz - ing\_\_\_ hap-pens; this is where

This is where a - maz - ing\_\_\_ hap-pens; this is where

God steps\_\_\_\_ in;\_\_\_\_ this is the place\_\_\_\_

God steps\_\_\_\_ in;\_\_\_\_ this is the place\_\_\_\_

40
where bro - ken dreams can live a-gain. When you're to the
where bro - ken dreams can live a-gain. When you're to the
Am7
G
C
D sus
D

42
end of hope, no-where else for you to go,
end of hope, no-where else for you to go,
G
D
F♯
G
B

44
wel-come to a place of sec-ond chanc - es; this is where a-maz-ing
wel-come to a place of sec-ond chanc - es; this is where a-maz-ing
Am7
G/C
Dsus
D
53
46
hap - pens.
Noth - ing's ev - er found un -
hap - pens.
f
Ah.
f
Gsus
G
cresc.
Dm(add4)/F
C/E
f

less it first\_\_\_ is lost.\_\_\_ There's not a res - ur-rec - tion, with-

There's not a res - ur-rec - tion.\_\_\_

Cm6/E♭    G/D    A2/C♯

out there is\_\_\_ a cross.\_\_\_ This is where a-

*cresc.* Ah.\_\_\_ This is where a-

*cresc.*

*f*

G/C    D sus

maz - ing hap-pens; this is where God steps in; this is the place

maz - ing hap-pens; this is where God steps in; this is the place

where bro - ken dreams can live a - gain.

where bro - ken dreams can live a - gain.

When you're to the end of___ hope,___ no-where else for

When you're to the end of___ hope,___ no-where else for

you to go,___ wel - come to___ a place___ of sec - ond

you to go,___ wel - come to___ a place___ of sec - ond

chanc - es;_____ this is where a-maz - ing hap - pens.____

chanc - es;_____ this is where a-maz - ing hap - pens.____

E sus    E    A

F♯m    D    A/C♯

54

When you're to the    end of___ hope,___    no-where else for

When you're to the    end of___ hope,___    no-where else for

B m  C♯m⁷    F♯m    E    A

65

you to go,___ oh, wel - come to___ a place___ of sec - ond

you to go,___ wel - come to___ a place___ of sec - ond

E/G♯  A/C♯  B m7  A/D

67

chanc - es;___ this is where a - maz - ing hap - pens.___ Oh,

chanc - es;___ this is where a - maz - ing hap - pens.___

E sus  E  A  D/F♯

this is where a-maz - ing hap - pens._____ Oh,_____

this is where a-maz - ing hap - pens._____

this is where a-maz - ing hap - pens._____

# Your Throne Will Last Forever

Words and Music by
RANDY PHILLIPS and JOHN RAGSDALE
*Arr. by Geron Davis
and Bradley Knight*

**56** Driving Rock ♩ = 126

1. Hear the might-y thun-der, an ar-my with-out

2. See His eyes of fi-re, the Lamb is now a

10

num-ber, danc-ing on\_\_ the king - doms of \_\_ this

Li-on, bring-ing jus - tice in\_\_ His nail\_\_ scarred\_\_

F    Eb/F

13

world.\_\_ See their ban - ner wav - in',

hand, Bring-ing down our plac - es,

Bb/F    F    Eb2

17

hear the name they're prais - in'.

the hum - ble sing His prais - es,\_\_

Bb

**19**

He is___ the King of kings, and He's the

'cause the King has re - turned___ to rule

F    E♭2

**56** **59**

**21**

Lord___ of lords.___

___ this___ land.___

CHOIR *unis.*
*f*
So pre - pare
*f*

B♭

23
Pre - pare the way
on a
the way
for the
An - cient of Days
A♭2
B♭2
25
white horse.
And as He starts to ride, hear the peo-
on a white horse.
F (no3)
A♭2

28
57
60
ple cry!
Hear the peo - ple cry!
Your throne
B♭
cresc.
30
SOLO may ad lib
will last for-ev - er,
through-out the end - less age.
F (no 3)
E♭
A♭

132

Ev - 'ry knee bow down, ev - 'ry tongue

say it loud: Your throne, Your throne will last

for - ev - er!

40
58
(page 127, meas. 7)
2
Your throne
F E E♭
E♭2
43
will last for-ev - er, through-out the end - less age.
F(no3)
E♭
A♭
46
Ev - 'ry knee bow down, ev - 'ry tongue
B♭
F(no3)

say it loud:\_\_\_ Your throne,\_\_\_ Your throne\_\_\_ will last

C m⁷           D♭²

for-ev - er!\_\_\_

E♭²           C   E♭ C    E♭ F E E♭

SOLO
*f*

Let Your King-dom\_\_\_ come, let Your will be\_\_\_ done. Right now,

*Drums*

CHOIR *unis.*
SOLO *may ad lib*

Right now!_____ Let Your King-dom____ come, let Your will be____ done.

Right now, Right now! Let Your King - dom____ come,

let Your will be____ done. Right now, Right now!

66
Let Your King - dom come, let Your will be done.
F (no 3)
E♭/F
sim.
68
Right now, Right now! Let Your King-dom come,
B♭/F
B♭/F
F (no 3)
71
62
let Your will be done. Right now, Right now!
E♭/F
B♭/F
B♭/F
cresc.

Lyrics:
Let Your King-dom___ come, let Your will be___ done. Right now,

Right now! Let Your King-dom___ come, let Your will be___ done.

Right now, Right now! Your throne will last___ for-ev-

-er, through-out the end - less age.____ Ev-'ry knee

bow____ down,____ ev- 'ry tongue____ say it loud:____ Your throne,

Your throne____ will last.____ Your throne

will last\_\_\_ for-ev - er, through-out the end - less age.\_\_\_

Ev - 'ry knee bow\_\_\_ down,\_\_\_ ev - 'ry tongue

\_\_\_ say it loud:\_\_\_ Your throne,\_\_\_ Your throne\_\_\_ will last,\_\_\_

97
Your throne,
Your throne
will last,
E♭2
D♭2/F
99
Your throne,
Your throne
will last,
for - ev -
E♭2/G
D♭2/A♭
E♭2/B♭
E♭2
102
- er!
Yeah!
(16)
C
E♭
C
A♭
A
B♭
B
C
A♭
G
F (no3)
(16)